BEST. JOKES. EVER.

JOKES for KIDS

CHANTELLE GRACE

BroadStreet
PUBLISHING

BroadStreet Kids
Racine, Wisconsin, USA

BroadStreet Kids is an imprint of BroadStreet Publishing Group, LLC.
Broadstreetpublishing.com

BEST.JOKES.EVER.

ISBN 978-1-4245-5464-5
Content compiled by Chantelle Grace.

Design by Chris Garborg | garborgdesign.com
Editorial services by Michelle Winger | literallyprecise.com

Printed in the United States of America.

18   19   20   21   22   23   7   6   5   4

Author Bio

CHANTELLE GRACE is a witty wordsmith who loves music, art, and competitive games. She is fascinated by God's intricate design of the human body. As she works her way through medical school, she knows it's important to share the gift of laughter with those around her. When she's not studying abroad, she makes her home in Prior Lake, Minnesota.

TABLE OF CONTENTS .....

Education Entertainment   6

Geography Giggles   9

Pirate Play   12

Musical Madness   15

Food Funnies   18

Animal Antics   24

Space Slapstick   40

Nature Nonsense   43

Sports Sillies   46

Transportation Thrills   49

Home Hysteria   52

History Hilarity   55

Fairytale Fun   58

Media Merriment   64

Weather Wit   67

Dinosaur Drama   70

Holiday Humor   76

Animal Antics... Again   79

Medical Mischief   88

Legal Laughs   94

EDUCATION ENTERTAINMENT

Why was the math book sad?

Because it had too many problems.

Why were the teacher's eyes crossed?

She couldn't control her pupils.

Why did the boy eat his homework?

Because his teacher told him it was a piece of cake.

Which weighs more, a ton of feathers
or a ton of bricks?

Neither, they both weigh a ton.

What did the janitor say when he
jumped out of the closet?

"Supplies!"

Why was the student's
report card wet?

It was below C level.

What did one pencil say
to the other pencil?

"You're looking sharp."

Where do pencils go on vacation?

Pennsylvania.

Why did the girl bring lipstick and eye shadow to school?

She had a make-up test.

Why should you take a pencil to bed?

To draw the curtains.

How many books can you put in an empty backpack?

One. After that, it's not empty.

How many letters are in The Alphabet?

There are 11 letters in "The Alphabet."

The turtle took two chocolates to Texas to teach Thomas to tie his boots. How many t's are in that?

There are two t's in that.

GEOGRAPHY GIGGLES

Teacher: Where is the English Channel?

Student: I don't know. My TV doesn't pick it up.

What is the capital of Alaska?

Come on, Juneau this one.

What rock group has four men that don't sing?

Mount Rushmore.

What city cheats at exams?

Peking.

What is the capital of Washington?

The W.

What did Delaware?

Her New Jersey.

What is the fastest country
in the world?

Rush-a.

Teacher: What can you tell me
about the Dead Sea?

*Student: I didn't even know
it was sick.*

What are the Great Plains?

The 747, Concorde, and F-16.

What has five eyes and is lying
on the water?

The Mississippi River.

What did one US flag say to the other?

Nothing, it just waved.

What do you find in the middle
of nowhere?

The letter "h."

What do you call a nutty dog
in Australia?

A dingo-ling.

What birds are found in Portugal?

Portu-geese.

How do you repair a car in Scotland?

With scotch tape.

PIRATE PLAY

Why are pirates called pirates?

Cause they arrrrr.

Why does it take pirates so long
to learn the alphabet?

Because they spend years at C.

Why couldn't the pirate play cards?

Because he was sitting on the deck.

How much did the pirate pay
for his earrings?

A buccaneer.

What is a pirate's favorite subject?

Arrrrrrt.

How much did the pirate pay for his hook and peg leg?

An arm and a leg.

Why can't you take a picture of a pirate with a wooden leg?

Because a wooden leg doesn't take pictures.

What do you call a pirate with two eyes and two legs?

A rookie.

What is a pirate's favorite country?

Arrrrrrgentina.

What grades did the pirate get in school?

High C's.

Why didn't the pirate's phone work?

Because he left it off the hook.

What are pirates afraid of?

The darrrrrk.

What do you call a pirate that skips class?

Captain Hooky.

Why didn't the pirate go to the movies?

Because it was arrrrrr rated.

What has eight legs and eight eyes?

Eight pirates.

MUSICAL MADNESS

How do you make a band stand?

Take their chairs away.

What do little penguins sing when their father brings fish home for dinner?

Freeze a Jolly Good Fellow.

What do you get if you cross a sweet potato and a jazz musician?

A yam session.

Why is a piano so hard to open?

Because the keys are on the inside.

What's the most musical bone?

The trom-bone.

Why was the musician arrested?

Because she got in treble.

Why is slippery ice like music?

If you don't C sharp; you'll B flat.

What was the result when a piano fell down a mine shaft?

A-flat minor.

What was stolen from the music store?

The lute.

How do you make a tissue dance?

Put a little boogey in it.

What do you get when you cross
a fridge with a radio?

Cool music.

Why did Mozart get rid of his chickens?

They kept saying Bach, Bach.

Why couldn't the athlete listen
to her music?

Because she broke the record.

What type of music are balloons
afraid of?

Pop music.

FOOD FUNNIES

When do you go at red and stop at green?

When you're eating a watermelon.

How did the farmer mend his pants?

With cabbage patches.

Why did the man lose his job at the orange juice factory?

He couldn't concentrate.

What do you repair a tomato with?

Tomato Paste.

What did the hamburger name
his daughter?

Patty.

What did the grape do when it got
stepped on?

It let out a little wine.

Why do sharks live in salt water?

Because pepper makes them sneeze.

What did Bacon say to Tomato?

"Lettuce get together."

What is a bubbles least favorite drink?

Soda POP.

What did one plate say to the other?

"Dinner's on me."

What is black, white, green, and bumpy?

A pickle wearing a tuxedo.

What's the best thing to put into a pie?

Your teeth.

Patron: Waiter, this food tastes kind of funny.

Waiter: Then why aren't you laughing?

Why do the French like to eat snails?

Because they don't like fast food.

Why did the fisherman put peanut
butter into the sea?

To go with the jellyfish.

Why shouldn't you tell an egg a joke?

Because it might crack up.

What did the baby corn say
to its mom?

"Where is pop corn?"

What do you call candy that is stolen?

Hot chocolate.

What kind of nuts always seems
to have a cold?

Cashews.

Waiter, will my pizza be long?

"No sir, it will be round."

What is green and sings?

Elvis Parsley.

Why did the banana go to the doctor?

Because it wasn't peeling well.

What candy do you eat
on the playground?

Recess pieces.

What do dwarves
make sandwiches with?

Shortbread.

Why shouldn't you tell a secret
on a farm?

Because corn has ears.

What is a pretzel's favorite dance?

The Twist.

What are twins' favorite fruit?

Pears.

If a crocodile makes shoes,
what does a banana make?

Slippers.

What do you give to a sick lemon?

Lemon aid.

ANIMAL ANTICS

What does a shark like to eat
with peanut butter?

A jellyfish.

What happened to the dog
that swallowed a firefly?

It barked with de-light.

What kind of key opens a banana?

A monkey.

Why do gorillas have big nostrils?

Because they have big fingers.

Who's the penguin's favorite Aunt?

Aunt-Arctica.

What is a shark's favorite sci-fi show?

Shark Trek.

How does a lion greet the other animals in the field?

"Pleased to eat you."

How do you know that carrots are good for your eyesight?

Rabbits never wear glasses.

Why don't dogs make good dancers?

Because they have two left feet.

What do cats eat for breakfast?

Mice Crispies.

What did the farmer call the cow
that had no milk?

An udder failure.

What do you get if you cross a chicken
with a cow?

Roost beef.

Why did the monkey like the banana?

Because it had appeal.

When is a dog not a dog?

When it is pure bred.

What's white, furry, and shaped like
a tooth?

A molar bear.

How do bears keep their den cool
in summer?

They use bear conditioning.

Why don't you have to tell an elephant a secret more than once?

Because elephants never forget.

What's a penguin's favorite salad?

Iceberg lettuce.

What do you call a solitary shark?

A lone shark.

What dog keeps the best time?

A watch dog.

Why didn't the boy believe the tiger?

He thought it was a lion.

What do you get from a pampered cow?

Spoiled milk.

What do you get when you cross fish and an elephant?

Swimming trunks.

Why is a fish easy to weigh?

Because it has its own scales.

Why was the rabbit so upset?

She was having a bad hare day.

What did the banana say to the monkey?

Nothing, bananas can't talk.

What happens when a frog parks in a no-parking space?

It gets toad away.

What does a twenty-pound mouse say to a cat?

"Here kitty, kitty, kitty."

What is a frog's favorite exercise?

Jumping Jacks.

What type of horses only go out at night?

Nightmares.

What do you call a bear with no teeth?

A gummy bear.

What snakes are found on cars?

Windshield vipers.

What do you get when a chicken lays an egg on top of a barn?

An eggroll.

Why are frogs so happy?

They eat whatever bugs them.

What did the pony say when it had a sore throat?

"I'm a little hoarse."

Why are elephants so wrinkled?

They take too long to iron.

When is a well-dressed lion like a weed?

When he's a dandelion.

What do monkeys do for laughs?

They tell jokes about people.

What do you call a bear with no ears?

B.

What has 12 legs, six eyes, three tails, and can't see?

Three blind mice.

What is an owl's favorite subject?

Owl-gebra.

Why did the snake cross the road?

To get to the other ssssssside.

What is a cat's favorite color?

Purr-ple.

What fish only swims at night?

A starfish.

Why are teddy bears never hungry?

They are always stuffed.

How do you get down off an elephant?

You don't, you get down off a duck.

Why did the penguin cross the road?

To go with the floe.

What sport don't you want to play
with an elephant?

Squash.

What happened to the lost cattle?

Nobody's herd.

What's gray, squeaky, and hangs around
in caves?

Stalagmice.

Why did the elephant color himself
different colors?

So he could hide in the crayon box.

What do you call an owl
with a deep voice?

A growl.

Where do penguins go to the movies?

At the dive-in.

What do you get when you cross
a snake and a pie?

A pie-thon.

How does a penguin make pancakes?

With its flippers.

Why can't you shock cows?

They've herd it all.

Why are there some fish at the bottom
of the ocean?

Because they dropped out of school.

How many tickles does it take to make
an octopus laugh?

Ten-tickles.

How do bees get to school?

By school buzz.

Where do polar bears vote?

The North Poll.

What do you get if you cross a stuffed bear with a pig?

A teddy boar.

Why are snakes hard to fool?

You can't pull their leg.

Why didn't the chicken cross the road?

Because there was a KFC on the other side.

Why did the owl say, "Tweet, tweet"?

Because she didn't give a hoot.

What animal has more lives than a cat?

Frogs—they croak every night.

Why did the boy stand behind
the horse?

*He thought he might get a kick
out of it.*

Why did the chicken cross the road?

To show everyone he wasn't chicken.

What do you get when you cross
a sheep and a honey bee?

Bah-humbug.

How do you raise a baby elephant?

With a fork lift.

What do you call a dancing sheep?

A baa-lerina.

Where do hamsters come from?

Hamsterdam.

Someone said you sounded like an owl.

"Who?"

What is gray and blue and very big?

An elephant holding its breath.

Where do penguins go to dance?

The snow ball.

What do you give a sick horse?

Cough stirrup.

What is a baby owl after
it is six days old?

Seven days old.

What do penguins have for lunch?

Icebergers.

Two flies are on the porch.
Which one is an actor?

The one on the screen.

What is the biggest ant in the world?

An elephant.

Why was the baby ant confused?

Because all of his uncles were ants.

Why do bees have sticky hair?

Because they have honeycombs.

What animals are the best pets?

Cats, because they are purr-fect.

What are caterpillars afraid of?

Dogger-pillars.

What do you call a great dog detective?

Sherlock Bones.

What do you call a sheep that is always quiet?

A shhhheep.

What do you call young dogs who play in the snow?

Slush puppies.

What do you call a crate of ducks?

A box of quackers.

What type of markets do dogs avoid?

Flea markets.

Why did the birdie go
to the candy store?

It wanted a tweet.

Why do male deer need braces?

Because they have buck teeth.

What's yellow, weighs 1,000 pounds,
and sings?

Two 500-pound canaries.

SPACE SLAPSTICK

What did Mars say to Saturn?

"Give me a ring sometime."

When is the moon the heaviest?

When it's full.

When do astronauts eat?

At launch time.

**What type of songs
do the planets sing?**

Nep-tunes.

What is an astronaut's favorite key
on a keyboard?

The space bar.

How do you get a baby astronaut
to sleep?

You rocket.

What's the astronaut's favorite candy
bar?

A Mars bar.

Why did the sun want to go to college?

To brighten its future.

Where did the astronaut park
her spaceship?

A parking meteor.

What was the first animal in space?

The cow that jumped over the moon.

What did the alien say to the cat?

"Take me to your litter."

Why did the astronaut retire?

He got spaced out.

How do astronauts eat
their ice cream?

In floats.

How does one astronaut on the moon
tell another astronaut that he is sorry?

He Apollogises.

NATURE NONSENSE

Where does a tree store their stuff?

In their trunk.

What kind of shorts do clouds wear?

Thunderwear.

Why did the tree go to the dentist?

It needed a root canal.

What falls but never hits the ground?

The temperature.

What do you call an attractive volcano?

Lavable.

What did the tree wear
to the pool party?

Swimming trunks.

What did the cloud say
to the lightning bolt?

"You're shocking."

What did the beaver say to the tree?

"It's been nice gnawing you."

Why did the leaf go to the doctor?

It was feeling green.

What is a tree's least favorite month?

Septimber.

What did the tornado say
to the sports car?

"Want to go for a spin?"

What kind of tree can fit into your
hand?

A palm tree.

How do trees get on the internet?

They log in.

What's a tornado's favorite game?

Twister.

How do hurricanes see?

With one eye.

SPORTS SILLIES

How do baseball players stay cool?

They sit next to their fans.

What is a cheerleader's favorite food?

Cheerios.

Why is basketball such a messy sport?

Because everyone dribbles on the floor.

You can serve it, but you can't eat it. What is it?

A volleyball.

Why did the soccer player bring string
to the game?

He wanted to tie the score.

Why is a baseball team similar
to a muffin?

They both depend on the batter.

Why do golfers wear two pairs of pants?

In case they get a hole in one.

Why did the man run around his bed?

*Because he wanted to catch up
on his sleep.*

What do you call a boomerang
that doesn't work?

A stick.

Why did the football coach go
to the bank?

He wanted his quarter back.

What is harder to catch the faster
you run?

Your breath.

Why is tennis such a loud sport?

The players raise a racquet.

Why did Tarzan spend so much time
on the golf course?

He was perfecting his swing.

Why did the ballerina quit?

Because it was tutu hard.

TRANSPORTATION THRILLS

What has four wheels and flies?

A garbage truck.

Which driver never gets a parking ticket?

A screw-driver.

What happened to the wooden car with a wooden engine?

It wooden go.

Which part of a car is always tired?

The exhaust pipe.

What is a car's favorite type of shoes?

Vans.

What do you call a person who draws animations on vehicles?

A car-toonist.

What song does the car like to play?

A car-tune.

What did the jack say to the car?

"Can I give you a lift?"

Why is an old car similar to a baby toy?

They both rattle.

What part of the car is the laziest?

The wheels, because they are always tired.

When do cars get the most flat tires?

When there's a fork in the road.

What car can drive over the water?

Any car that goes across a bridge.

Who earns a living driving their customers away?

A taxi driver.

HOME HYSTERIA

Did you hear the joke about the roof?

Never mind, it's over your head.

What can go up a chimney down,
but can't go down a chimney up?

An umbrella.

What goes up and down but does
not move?

Stairs.

What did one toilet say to the other?

"You look a bit flushed."

What did one wall say to the other wall?

"I'll meet you at the corner."

Why did the boy throw the clock
out the window?

He wanted to see time fly.

When is a door not a door?

When it is ajar.

Why do fluorescent lights hum?

Because they forgot the words.

Why did the house go to the doctor?

Because it had a window pane.

What gives you the power
to walk through walls?

A door.

What gets wetter the more it dries?

A towel.

How do you warm up a room after it's been painted?

Give it a second coat.

Why was the broom late?

It over swept.

What has one head, one foot, and four legs?

A bed.

What did the blanket say to the bed?

"Don't worry, I've got you covered."

HISTORY HILARITY

What happened when the wheel
was invented?

It caused a revolution.

Why were the early days of history
called the dark ages?

Because there were so many knights.

How were the first Americans like ants?

They also lived in colonies.

What does the Statue of Liberty
stand for?

It can't sit down.

Where did the pilgrims land when they came to America?

On their feet.

How did the Vikings send secret messages?

By norse code.

Who invented fractions?

Henry the 1/4th.

What did they do at the Boston Tea Party?

I don't know, I wasn't invited.

What's purple and 5000 miles long?

The grape wall of China.

What did Mason say to Dixon?

"We've got to draw the line here."

Who made King Arthur's round table?

Sir-Cumference.

What do Alexander the Great and Kermit the Frog have in common?

The same middle name.

Where was the Declaration of Independence signed?

At the bottom.

Why did the pioneers cross the country in covered wagons?

Because they didn't want to wait forty years for a train.

How was the Roman Empire cut in half?

With a pair of Caesars.

FAIRYTALE FUN

How do you find a princess?

You follow the foot prince.

Why do dragons sleep during the day?

So they can fight knights.

What did the damsel in distress say when her photos did not show up?

"Someday my prints will come."

What kind of car does Mickey Mouse's wife drive?

A Minnie van.

What do you call a rabbit with fleas?

Bugs Bunny.

What did Winnie the Pooh say
to his agent?

"Show me the honey!"

Why did Mickey Mouse take a trip
into space?

He wanted to find Pluto.

Why can't you give Elsa a balloon?

Because she'll let it go.

Why are there no planes where Peter
Pan lives?

*Because there is a sign that says
"Never Neverland."*

What did Nala say to Simba during the stampede?

"Move fasta."

Why does Alice ask so many questions?

Because she is in Wonder land.

What does Pooh Bear call his girlfriend?

Hunny.

What is Peter Pan's favorite restaurant?

Wendy's.

Where can you find a little mermaid?

Under the sea.

Who is Wall-E's cousin?

Floor-E.

What does Ariel like on her toast?

Mermalade.

What did Woody say to Buzz Lightyear?

A lot. There were three movies.

Why was Cinderella so bad at soccer?

Because she was always running away from the ball, she kept losing her shoes, and she had a pumpkin for a coach.

Why did Arlo help Spot cross the road?

Because he was "The Good Dinosaur."

Why did Sleepy take firewood to bed with him?

He wanted to sleep like a log.

Why did Sven try to eat Olaf's nose?

Because he doesn't carrot all.

What is Mickey Mouse's favorite sport?

Minnie-golf.

What do you call a fairy who doesn't bathe for a year?

Stinker Bell.

What do Bongo and Lulubelle need to live?

Just the bear necessities.

What is Grumpy's favorite fruit?

Sour Grapes.

What kind of blush does Mulan wear?

Mulan Rouge.

What do you get when you cross
Winnie-the-Pooh and a skunk?

Winnie the P.U.

Why does Snow White always treat each
of the Seven Dwarfs equally?

Because she's the fairest of them all.

Where did Captain Hook get his hook?

From the second hand store.

MEDIA MERRIMENT

What do you say when you lose
a wii game?

"I want a wii-match."

What never asks questions but receives
a lot of answers?

The phone.

What kind of dance did the computer
go to?

A disc-o dance.

What's the difference between a TV
and a newspaper?

Ever tried swatting a fly with a TV?

What did the spider do
on the computer?

Made a website.

What did the computer do
at lunchtime?

Had a byte.

What does a baby computer call
his father?

Data.

Why did the computer keep sneezing?

It had a virus.

What is a computer virus?

A terminal illness.

Why was the computer cold?

It left its Windows open.

Why was there a bug in the computer?

Because it was looking for a byte to eat.

Why did the computer squeak?

Because someone stepped on its mouse.

What do you get when you cross a computer and a life guard?

A screensaver.

Where do all the cool mice live?

In their mousepads.

WEATHER WIT

What goes up when the rain
comes down?

An umbrella.

Why do Eskimos do their laundry
in Tide?

Because it's too cold out-tide.

What season is it when you bounce
on a trampoline?

Spring.

Why do birds fly south for the winter?

It's quicker than walking.

What goes up and down
but doesn't move?

The temperature.

Why is England the wettest country?

*Because the queen has reigned there
for years.*

What did one volcano say to the other?

"I lava you."

What bow can't be tied?

A rainbow.

What happens when the fog disappears
in California?

UCLA.

How hot is it?

It's so hot, when I turned on the sprinkler, all I got was steam!

Who does everyone listen to, but no one believes?

The weatherman.

What is the opposite of a cold front?

A warm back.

Why was there thunder and lightning in the lab?

The scientists were brainstorming.

What do you do when it's raining cats and dogs?

Watch out for the poodles.

DINOSAUR DRAMA

What does a triceratops sit on?

Its tricera-bottom.

What do you call a sleeping dinosaur?

A dino-snore.

Why did the Archaeopteryx catch the worm?

Because it was an early bird.

What was T. Rex's favorite number?

Ate.

Why did the dinosaur get in bed?

Because he was tired.

What do you call a fossil that doesn't
ever want to work?

Lazy bones.

What do you get when dinosaurs crash
their cars?

Tyrannosaurus wrecks.

What did the dinosaur say after
the car crash?

I'm-so-saurus.

What do you call it when a dinosaur
makes a goal?

A dino-score.

What do you call a dinosaur
with no eyes?

Do-ya-think-he-saw-us.

What's the best way to talk
to a Tyrannosaur?

Long distance.

What do you say when you meet
a two-headed dinosaur?

"Hello, hello."

Is it true that a dinosaur won't attack
if you hold a tree branch?

It depends on how fast you carry it.

What makes more noise
than a dinosaur?

Two dinosaurs.

What do you call a Stegosaurus
with carrots in its ears?

Anything you want; it can't hear you.

What's better than a talking dinosaur?

A spelling bee.

What do you call a dinosaur that never gives up?

Try-Try-Try-ceratops.

What kind of dinosaur can you ride in a rodeo?

A bronco-saurus.

What do you get when you cross a dinosaur with fireworks?

Dino-mite.

When can three giant dinosaurs get under one umbrella and not get wet?

When it's not raining.

Which type of dinosaur could jump higher than a house?

Any kind. A house can't jump.

What do you do if you find a blue Ichthyosaur?

Cheer him up.

Why don't dinosaurs ever forget?

Because no one ever tells them anything.

Do you know how long dinosaurs should be fed?

Exactly the same as short dinosaurs.

What do you need to know to teach a dinosaur tricks?

More than the dinosaur.

Where was the dinosaur when the sun went down?

In the dark.

What happened when the dinosaur took the train home?

She had to bring it back.

How do you know if there's a dinosaur under your bed?

Your nose hits the ceiling.

Why was the dinosaur afraid of the ocean?

Because there was something fishy about it.

What do you call a dinosaur that left its armor out in the rain?

A stegosaurust.

How do you know if there's a dinosaur in your refrigerator?

Look for footprints in the pizza.

HOLIDAY HUMOR

What is a cow's favorite day?

Moo-years day.

What did the light bulb say to her man on Valentine's Day?

"I love you watts and watts."

Where does the Easter bunny get his breakfast?

IHOP.

How does the Easter bunny stay in shape?

Lots of eggsercise.

What was the most popular dance in 1776?

Indepen-dance.

What do you call a fake stone in Ireland?

A sham rock.

Why is St. Patrick's Day most frogs' favorite holiday?

Because they are already wearing green.

What's a four-leaf clover's favorite dance?

The shamrock shake.

What is the fear of Santa Claus called?

Claustrophobia.

What nationality is Santa Claus?

North Polish.

What does Tarzan sing at Christmas?

Jungle Bells.

Why does Santa have a garden?

So he can hoe, hoe, hoe.

What is a parent's favorite Christmas carol?

Silent Night.

Why is it cold on Christmas Day?

Because it's in Decembrrrrrr.

ANIMAL ANTICS... AGAIN

Why did the pig become an actor?

Because he was a ham.

How do you save a deer during hunting season?

You hang on for deer life.

When does a dog go "moo"?

When it is learning a new language.

Why do seagulls fly over the sea?

Because if they flew over the bay, they would be bagels.

What kind of pigs know karate?

Pork chops.

Who stole the soap?

The robber ducky.

What do you call a happy Lassie?

A jolly collie.

How do Hispanic sheep say Merry Christmas?

Fleece Navidad.

What kind of ties do pigs wear?

Pigs-ties.

Where does a peacock go when
it loses its tail?

A re-tail store.

What's worse than raining cats
and dogs?

Hailing taxis.

What kind of cats like to go bowling?

Alley cats.

Why did the pig take a bath?

The farmer said, "Hogwash."

What do you call a deer with no eyes?

I have no I-deer.

What do you call a deer with no eyes
and no legs?

Still no eye-deer.

Why does a flamingo stand on one leg?

Because if he lifted that leg off the ground, he would fall down.

How did the little Scottish dog feel when he saw a monster?

He was terrier-fied.

What do ducks watch on TV?

Duckumentaries.

How many sheep does it take to knit a sweater?

Don't be silly; sheep can't knit.

What do you call cattle with a sense of humor?

Laughing stock.

Why don't sharks like fast food?

Because they can't catch it.

What do you get if you cross a frog
and a dog?

A croaker spaniel.

What animal sounds like a sheep
but isn't?

A baaaa-boon.

Where do Eskimos train their dogs?

In the mush room.

Why was the sheep pulled over
on the freeway?

Because she did a ewe-turn.

What did the shark say to the whale?

"What are you blubbering about?"

How do monkeys get down the stairs?

They slide down the bananaster.

What do you get if you cross an angry sheep and a grumpy cow?

An animal that's in a baaaaaaad mooooooood.

What is a frog's favorite hot drink?

Hot croak-o.

How do chickens bake a cake?

From scratch.

What do you give a sick pig?

Oinkment.

What is a cat's favorite song?

Three Blind Mice.

What dog loves to take bubble baths?

A shampoodle.

Why are elephants so poor?

Because they work for peanuts.

What did the doctor say when the monkey cut off his tail?

"It won't be long now."

What do you call a cow with two legs?

Lean beef.

What do you call a cow with no legs?

Ground beef.

What goes dot-dot-croak,
dot-dash-croak?

A morse toad.

What do you call a fish without an eye?

A fsh.

What's black and white, black and white,
and black and white?

A panda bear rolling down a hill.

What do you call a snake with a great
personality?

A snake charmer.

Why did the piece of gum cross
the road?

It was stuck to the chicken's foot.

What do you get if you cross a cocker spaniel, a poodle, and a rooster?

Cockerpoodledoo.

If fruit comes from a fruit tree, where does chicken come from?

A poul-tree.

Where do frogs leave their hats and coats?

In the croakroom.

How do you stop an elephant from charging?

Take away its credit card.

MEDICAL MISCHIEF

Why did the bee go to the doctor?

Because it had hives.

What does a dentist call his X-rays?

Tooth-pics.

What does a sick lemon need?

Lemon aid.

What does a doctor give an elephant who's going to be sick?

Plenty of room.

Why didn't the girl tell the doctor
that she ate some glue?

Her lips were sealed.

What did the nose say to the finger?

"Stop picking on me."

What do you give a dog with a fever?

*Ketchup. It's the best thing
for a hot dog.*

Why did the banana go to the doctor?

It was not peeling well.

Why did the boy tiptoe past the
medicine cabinet?

*He didn't want to wake
the sleeping pills.*

What kind of button won't unbutton?

A bellybutton.

When is the best time to go
to the dentist?

At tooth-hurty.

Why did the computer go
to the doctor?

Because it had a virus.

What did one eyeball say
to the other eyeball?

*"Between you and me
something smells."*

Why did the cookie go to the hospital?

He felt crummy.

What is a happy doctor's favorite
blood type?

B positive.

What did the judge say to the dentist?

"Do you swear to pull the tooth, the whole tooth, and nothing but the tooth?"

Why did the king go to the dentist?

To get his teeth crowned.

What does a dentist do during an earthquake?

He braces himself.

What did the tooth say to the dentist as she was leaving?

"Fill me in when you get back."

What is a dentist's favorite animal?

A molar bear.

Has your tooth stopped hurting yet?

I don't know, the dentist kept it.

What did the dentist get for an award?

A little plaque.

When does a doctor get mad?

When he runs out of patients.

Why did the pillow go to the doctor?

He was feeling all stuffed up.

Where does a boat go when it's sick?

To the dock.

What did one tonsil say
to the other tonsil?

*"Get dressed up; the doctor
is taking us out."*

Patient: Doctor, sometimes I feel like I'm invisible.

Doctor: Who said that?

Patient: Doctor, Doctor I think I'm a moth.

Doctor: Get out of my light.

Patient: Doctor, I keep hearing a ringing sound.

Doctor: Then answer the phone.

Did you hear the one about the germ?

Never mind, I don't want to spread it around.

How do you cure a headache?

Put your head through a window and the pane will disappear.

LEGAL LAUGHS

What did the judge say when the skunk walked in the court room?

"Odor in the court."

What do prisoners use to call each other?

Cellphones.

What do lawyers wear to court?

Lawsuits.

Why did the picture go to jail?

Because it was framed.

What four letters will frighten a burglar?

O I C U.

What is it that even the most careful lawyers overlook?

Their nose.

Did you hear about the robbery last night?

Two clothes pins held up a sweater.

What do you call an underwater spy?

James Pond.

What did the lawyer name his daughter?

Sue.

Why did the policeman go to the baseball game?

He heard someone had stolen a base.

Why did the book join the police?

He wanted to go undercover.

What do you get a man who has everything for his birthday?

A burglar alarm.

Why was the belt arrested?

Because it held up some pants.